The Big Book of Banking in India

From Past to Future

Vandana Verma

DIAMOND BOOKS

www.diamondbooks.in

Publisher	:	**Diamond Pocket Books (P) Ltd.** X-30, Okhla Industrial Area, Phase-II New Delhi-110020
Phone	:	011-40712200
E-mail	:	wecare@diamondbooks.in
Website	:	www.diamondbooks.in
Edition	:	2025
Printed By	:	Repro (India)

Preface

In a world driven by digital money, UPI transactions, and online savings accounts, it is more important than ever for young people to understand how banking works. This book, **"The Big Book of Banking in India – From Past to Future,"** is designed to make banking simple, relatable, and exciting for students.

From ancient trade practices to AI-driven banking apps, this book traces the incredible journey of India's banking system. Whether you're opening your first savings account or exploring careers in fintech, this book gives you the knowledge and confidence to take control of your financial future.

Aligned with the National Education Policy (NEP) 2020 and NCF 2023, the book introduces essential banking concepts through real-world examples, interactive activities, and visual tools. Each chapter is written in a crisp, student-friendly tone to spark curiosity and build practical financial awareness.

- Vandana Verma

Foreword

India is at the forefront of a digital banking revolution. With tools like Aadhaar, UPI, RuPay, and DigiLocker, the Indian banking system has become more accessible, secure, and inclusive than ever before. But how did we get here? And where are we heading next?

As a country preparing millions of young minds for the future, it is essential that our students are not just consumers of banking services but smart, informed users. This book is a small step toward building that financial literacy.

By understanding how banks operate, what services they offer, and how technology is reshaping finance, students can make informed choices, avoid financial risks, and even envision careers in this dynamic sector.

Whether you're a student, teacher, or parent, I hope this book inspires curiosity and clarity about the world of banking.

Table of Contents

Chapter 1

What Is a Bank?

Understanding the Basics

What Is a Bank?

Imagine a place where you can safely keep your money, borrow some when needed, or even earn extra just by saving. That place is called a bank.

A bank is a financial institution that accepts deposits from the public and lends money to individuals and businesses. Banks also help people transfer money, save securely, and access loans for their dreams—like education, buying a house, or starting a business.

Banks are everywhere today—online and offline. From the ATM at your street corner to the UPI app on your phone, the banking world is all around you. But what do banks actually do?

Core Functions of a Bank

Let's understand the main jobs a bank performs:

1. Accepting Deposits
Banks allow people to deposit their money into various types of accounts, such as savings accounts, current accounts, and fixed deposits. When you deposit money, the bank keeps it safe and pays you interest as a reward for keeping it there.

Example: If you deposit ₹10,000 in a savings account with 4% annual interest, you will earn ₹400 in a year.

2. Providing Loans
Banks lend money to people and businesses. These could be home loans, education loans, personal loans, or business loans. Borrowers repay the amount with interest.

Why do banks charge interest on loans? Because they are taking a risk and need to earn to pay depositors and cover expenses.

3. Money Transfers
Banks allow you to send and receive money. Whether you're using NEFT, IMPS, UPI, or a cheque, banks help move money securely from one person to another.

Example: Paying school fees online or sending money to your cousin in another city—all of it happens through banking channels.

4. Safekeeping and Advisory
Banks keep your valuables secure in lockers, help you plan your investments, and offer advice through financial services.

Why Are Banks Important in an Economy?

Banks are like the heart of an economy—they pump money across the system.

Here's how they help a country grow:

- **Promote savings**: Encourage people to save for the future.
- **Support businesses**: Provide loans to entrepreneurs and companies.
- **Create jobs:** Employ millions of people in banking, finance, and related sectors.
- **Enable development:** Finance projects like roads, bridges, schools, and hospitals.

Without banks, economic growth would be slower, and people would have limited options to manage their money safely.

Banking Terms Made Simple

Let's simplify some common banking words:

Term	Meaning
Deposit	Money you give to the bank for safekeeping
Withdrawal	Taking out money from your bank account
Interest	Extra money earned on savings or paid on loans
Loan	Money borrowed from a bank that must be repaid with interest
Account	A personal record with the bank showing your deposits and withdrawals

Types of Bank Accounts

Banks offer different kinds of accounts based on your needs:

1. **Savings Account** – Ideal for students and families; earns interest on

money saved.
2. **Current Account** – Used mostly by businesses; allows frequent transactions but no interest.
3. **Fixed Deposit (FD)** – Money is locked for a fixed period and earns higher interest.
4. **Recurring Deposit (RD)** – Deposit a fixed amount every month and get interest on total savings.

Life Without Banks – A Thought Experiment

What if banks didn't exist? Let's imagine:

- You'd hide your money at home, risking theft or loss.
- You'd borrow from moneylenders who might charge unfair interest.
- Businesses couldn't expand easily without access to credit.
- Sending money to someone in another city would be slow and risky.

Clearly, banks make life safer, faster, and more efficient!

Activity: "Bank or No Bank?"

Take a look at the following situations and decide: Could this happen with a bank or without a bank?

Scenario	With/Without Bank
Pay your school fee using a UPI app	With Bank
Hide ₹5,000 under your mattress	Without Bank
Your friend borrows ₹500 and promises to return next week	Without Bank
Open a joint savings account with your sibling	With Bank
Take a loan for your higher studies	With Bank
(Discuss your answers in class!)	

How Do Banks Make Money?

Banks are not charities—they are businesses. Here's how they earn:

- They pay you less interest on deposits than they charge on loans. The difference is their profit.
- They also charge fees for services like ATM withdrawals, cheque books, locker rentals, and account maintenance.
- Some banks invest in bonds, mutual funds, and earn returns on those investments.

Modern Banks: Not Just a Building

Today, you can use your mobile phone to check your balance, pay bills, and even apply for a loan. This is called digital banking, and it's changing how we interact with banks.

Apps like Google Pay, PhonePe, BHIM, and Paytm act like mini banks in your pocket. But they still work with actual banks behind the scenes.

Safety First – Banking the Smart Way

Even though banking is convenient, it must be done safely. Here's how:

- Never share your PIN, OTP, or passwords.
- Don't click on unknown links claiming "you won a lottery."
- If your card or phone is lost, inform the bank immediately.
- Always use official apps or websites for transactions.

Banks follow strict rules by the Reserve Bank of India (RBI) to protect customer data and money. But being alert is your responsibility too.

Real-World Examples

• Aarav (17) opened his first student savings account. He now tracks his expenses using mobile banking and saves for college.
• Meena's mother runs a small stitching business. With a microloan from a bank, she bought a new sewing machine and grew her income.
• Rahul's grandfather uses the bank locker to keep family gold and important documents safe.
Banks are for everyone, regardless of age, background, or occupation.

Quick Recap

• A bank is a place that manages money—safely stores, lends, and helps move it.
• Banks help individuals save and borrow, and support businesses and the economy.
• Accounts like savings, current, FD, RD serve different needs.
• Banks use interest and fees to earn income.
• Today's banks are increasingly digital and require cyber-smart users.

Think & Reflect

• Do you or your family have a bank account? What type is it?
• Have you ever visited a bank or used an ATM?
• What would your dream bank look like—what features would it have?

Let's Revise

• Banks = Safe place for money + loans + transfers
• Core Functions = Deposits, Loans, Transfers, Advisory
• Savings Account = Earn interest, ideal for students
• Always practice safe banking habits

Chapter 2

A Brief History of Banking in India

Banking in the Beginning – Ancient and Medieval India

Banking in India is not new. In fact, its roots go back over 2,000 years. Ancient Indian texts like the Manusmriti and Arthashastra mention financial transactions, lending, and interest.

In early times, people relied on moneylenders, traders, and temples for financial services. **Here's how:**

- Temples acted as custodians of wealth.
- Merchants gave out loans and helped transfer funds.
- Hundi system was used for sending money across regions (like a traditional cheque or promissory note).

This informal system helped trade flourish in ancient India and laid the foundation for banking practices.

The Colonial Era – British Rule and Early Modern Banks

The real transformation of Indian banking began in the 18th and 19th centuries, during British colonial rule.

First Banks in India

• **Bank of Hindustan** (est. 1770 in Calcutta): First bank in India, though it shut down in 1832.

• **Presidency Banks:**
  - **Bank of Bengal** (1809)
  - **Bank of Bombay** (1840)
  - **Bank of Madras** (1843)

These banks were set up under British charters to serve the government and facilitate trade for the East India Company.

Did You Know?
Each presidency bank had the power to print its own currency notes in its region until the RBI took over.

The Birth of the Reserve Bank of India (RBI) – 1935

In 1935, the Reserve Bank of India (RBI) was established as India's central bank.

Its roles:

• Control money supply and inflation
• Act as banker to the government and other banks
• Issue currency notes (except ₹1 notes, which are issued by the Government of India)

RBI became a strong pillar in regulating India's financial system. After independence, RBI was nationalized in 1949.

Post-Independence Era (1947–1990): Nation-Building Through Banks

After independence in 1947, India needed strong financial institutions to grow its economy and reduce poverty.
Nationalization of Banks – A Big Milestone
In 1969, Prime Minister Indira Gandhi nationalized 14 major private banks. The idea was to make banking more accessible to the poor and rural areas.

Again in 1980, 6 more private banks were nationalized.

✔ Goals of nationalization:

- Provide loans to farmers and small industries
- Spread banking in rural India
- Reduce dominance of private bankers

✔ Impact:

- More bank branches opened in villages
- Priority sector lending (like to agriculture) became mandatory
- Financial inclusion efforts began

Economic Liberalization – 1991 Onwards

In 1991, India faced an economic crisis. To fix it, the government introduced liberalization, privatization, and globalization reforms. This changed Indian banking forever.

Key Reforms in Banking:

1. Entry of Private Banks

Banks like ICICI Bank, HDFC Bank, Axis Bank, and IndusInd Bank were established. They brought modern technology, customer service, and competition.

2. Foreign Banks Came In

International banks like Citibank, HSBC, and Standard Chartered expanded in India.

3. Technology Adoption

Banks started using core banking systems, ATMs, and internet banking to improve speed and customer experience.

Case Study:

ICICI Bank, launched in 1994, became India's first bank to offer mobile banking, internet banking, and iMobile Pay—all under one roof.

Timeline Activity: Major Events in Indian Banking

Here's a visual timeline of key moments:

Year	Event
1770	Bank of Hindustan established
1809–1843	Presidency Banks set up
1935	RBI established
1949	RBI nationalized
1969	14 major banks nationalized
1980	6 more banks nationalized
1991	Economic reforms introduced
1994	New private sector banks like HDFC, ICICI

2001	Core banking and net banking began
2016	UPI launched, boosting digital payments
2022+	RBI begins exploring Digital Rupee (CBDC)

(Ask your teacher to print and display this timeline in class!)

The Rise of Digital Banking

In the 2000s, India's banking sector embraced digital tools. Now, you can:

- Send money instantly via UPI
- Pay bills using mobile apps
- Get loans or open accounts online

New-age tools like PhonePe, Paytm, and Google Pay are helping even small vendors and chaiwalas receive digital payments.

Think About It:

Your local vegetable seller accepting ₹20 through QR code is part of India's digital banking story!

Activity: Match the Milestone

Match the following events with the correct year:

Event	Year
UPI launched	A. 1935
Bank nationalization	B. 1969
Digital Rupee pilot	C. 2022
RBI established	D. 2016

Answers: 1–D, 2–B, 3–C, 4–A

Summary: Evolution at a Glance

Period	Key Features
Ancient & Medieval	Informal banking via merchants, hundis, temples
Colonial Era	Presidency Banks, RBI, note issuance
Post-Independence	Bank nationalization, rural focus, financial inclusion
Liberalization (1990s)	Private banks, foreign banks, tech integration
Digital Era	Mobile banking, UPI, digital wallets, neobanks

Think & Reflect

- Why do you think banks were nationalized in 1969?
- How would your grandparents have accessed banking services?
- What's one change in banking you've seen in your lifetime?

Let's Revise

- Indian banking evolved from informal trade networks to modern digital platforms.
- The RBI was founded in 1935 and became India's central bank.
- Bank nationalization in 1969 brought banking to rural India.
- Economic reforms in 1991 welcomed private and foreign banks.
- India is now a global leader in digital payments, thanks to innovations like UPI.

Chapter 3

Types of Banks in India

What Makes a Bank Different?

Not all banks are the same! Just like there are different types of schools—some teach general subjects, some are music or sports-focused—banks also have different purposes. Some help farmers, others help businesses, and some focus only on digital services.
In this chapter, we'll explore the main types of banks in India, what they do, and how they serve different people and needs.

1. Commercial Banks – Everyday Banking for Everyone

These are the most common banks. You'll find their branches in cities, towns, and even villages. They offer all the regular services like savings accounts, fixed deposits, loans, debit/credit cards, and online banking.

Types of Commercial Banks:

- **Public Sector Banks:** Owned mostly by the government.
  - **Examples:** State Bank of India (SBI), Bank of Baroda, Punjab National Bank (PNB)

- **Private Sector Banks:** Owned by private companies or individuals.
  - **Examples:** HDFC Bank, ICICI Bank, Axis Bank, Yes Bank

- **Foreign Banks:** International banks with branches in India.
  - **Examples:** Citibank, HSBC, Standard Chartered

Fun Fact: SBI is the largest bank in India with over 22,000 branches!

2. Cooperative Banks – Banking by the People, for the People

These banks are formed by groups of people or cooperatives, especially in small towns and rural areas. They focus on providing affordable credit to farmers, small shopkeepers, and local businesses.

Two Types:

- Urban Cooperative Banks (UCBs) – Found in towns and small cities.
- Rural Cooperative Banks – Operate in villages, mostly helping farmers.

✔ Features:

- Owned and managed by members
- Lower interest rates
- Easy loans for agriculture and small trade

Did You Know? Cooperative banks work on the principle of "one person, one vote"—everyone gets an equal say!

3. Regional Rural Banks (RRBs) – Reaching the Heart of India

RRBs were launched in 1975 to bring banking services to rural India. These banks help farmers, small traders, artisans, and workers in remote areas.

They are jointly owned by:

- Central Government (50%)
- State Government (15%)
- Sponsoring Bank (35%) – like SBI or Bank of Baroda

Services Offered:

- Savings and fixed deposits
- Crop loans
- Rural housing loans
- Support for self-help groups (SHGs)

Example: Prathama UP Gramin Bank serves rural parts of Uttar Pradesh.

Think About It: Imagine if RRBs didn't exist—how would rural communities access funds?

4. Small Finance Banks – Big Help in Small Packages

Small Finance Banks (SFBs) are newer, special banks launched to help people who don't usually get banking services—like street vendors, daily wage workers, and small farmers.

Launched: First one started in 2016
Services:

- Accept small deposits

- Provide micro-loans (small loans with short terms)
- Offer insurance and pension services
- Help with financial literacy

Examples:
- AU Small Finance Bank
- Equitas Small Finance Bank
- Ujjivan Small Finance Bank

Why They Matter: SFBs help millions of Indians start saving, get loans, and join the formal economy.

5. Payments Banks – Digital-Only Money Managers

Payments Banks are a new kind of bank created by RBI to promote digital banking. They don't offer all banking services like loans or credit cards but are perfect for basic transactions.

Features:
- Mobile-friendly
- Can hold up to ₹2 lakh per customer (as per RBI limit)
- No loans, but you can pay bills, transfer money, or recharge phones

Examples:
- Airtel Payments Bank
- India Post Payments Bank
- Paytm Payments Bank

Use Case: Many migrant workers and small vendors use Payments Banks to send and receive money digitally—no need to visit a physical bank!

6. Development Banks – Funding India's Growth

These banks don't deal with everyday banking. Instead, they fund large infrastructure, industry projects, and social development.

Key Development Banks in India:

- **SIDBI (Small Industries Development Bank of India):** Helps small and medium enterprises (SMEs)
- **NABARD (National Bank for Agriculture and Rural Development):** Supports agriculture and rural development
- **EXIM Bank**: Helps Indian exporters
- **National Housing Bank**: Promotes housing finance

SIDBI Example:

- Offers low-interest loans to small businesses for buying equipment, setting up factories, or hiring workers.

Visual Comparison: Types of Banks at a Glance

Type of Bank	Main Focus	Example
Commercial Bank	General public banking	SBI, HDFC, ICICI
Cooperative Bank	Community-based lending	Saraswat Bank, APCOB
Regional Rural Bank	Rural lending, agriculture support	Prathama UP Gramin Bank
Small Finance Bank	Micro-loans, financial inclusion	AU Bank, Ujjivan Bank
Payments Bank	Digital transactions, small savings	Paytm, India Post Payments Bank
Development Bank	Industrial, rural and infrastructure loans	SIDBI, NABARD, EXIM

Activity: Match the Bank Type

Match the bank with its purpose:

Bank	Purpose
SIDBI	A. Help exporters
NABARD	B. Fund small industries
EXIM Bank	C. Rural agriculture
Paytm Payments Bank	D. Mobile banking, small deposits

Answers: SIDBI – B, NABARD – C, EXIM – A, Paytm – D

Think & Reflect

- Which type of bank would be most useful to a farmer?
- Why do you think Payments Banks don't offer loans?
- Can a bank be both digital and cooperative in nature?

Let's Revise

- India has different types of banks to meet the needs of different people—farmers, students, businesses, and rural communities.
- Commercial Banks are the most common, offering full services.
- RRBs and Cooperative Banks focus on helping rural and small borrowers.
- Payments and Small Finance Banks promote digital banking and inclusion.
- Development Banks help build infrastructure and fund growth.

Chapter 4

Inside a Bank

Products & Services

When you walk into a bank—or even open a banking app—you're entering a world full of useful tools that can help you save money, borrow money, and make payments easily. But what exactly are all these services?

Why do they matter?

In this chapter, we'll take a tour of what happens inside a bank and explore the various products and services banks offer to customers like you, your family, and millions of others.

1. Bank Accounts – Your Money's Safe Home

Think of a bank account as a safe, organized place where you can store, save, and track your money. There are different types of bank accounts, each with its own purpose.

a) Savings Account

• Ideal for everyday people who want to save money and earn interest on it.
• You can deposit or withdraw money anytime.
• Most banks offer ATM cards, cheque books, and online access with this account.

Example: Riya deposits ₹5,000 each month into her savings account. At the end of the year, she earns interest on her savings—free money just for keeping it safe!

b) Current Account

• Meant for business people who need to do frequent and large transactions.
• No interest is usually paid.
• Allows unlimited transactions but may require a minimum balance.

c) Fixed Deposit (FD)

• You deposit a lump sum for a fixed time (e.g., 1 or 5 years).
• You earn higher interest than a savings account.
• You cannot withdraw before the term without a penalty.

Example: Kabir puts ₹50,000 in an FD for 2 years and earns 7% interest per year.

d) Recurring Deposit (RD)

• You deposit a fixed amount every month (say ₹1,000) for a fixed period.
• Great for people who want to save slowly but regularly.
• You earn interest like an FD.

2. Lending Services – Borrowing Made Easy

Sometimes, we need money for big things—like studying, buying a house, or starting a business. That's where banks come in with loans.

a) Personal Loan

- For general needs like medical bills, wedding, travel, etc.
- No need to show how you'll spend it.
- Interest rate is higher because it's an unsecured loan (no collateral).

b) Home Loan

- For buying or building a house.
- Usually a long-term loan (up to 30 years).
- Lower interest because the house is the collateral (security).

c) Education Loan

- Helps students pay for college or university.
- Includes tuition fees, living expenses, and travel.
- Repayment starts after studies are over (with a grace period).

d) Vehicle Loan

- For buying a bike or car.
- Usually needs a down payment.

Did You Know? Most loans are paid back in EMIs—Equated Monthly Instalments.

3. Cards – Swiping Made Simple

Cards make it easy to carry and spend money without using cash.

a) Debit Card

- Linked directly to your bank account.
- Money is deducted immediately when you swipe.

Example: You have ₹2,000 in your account and buy a pair of shoes for ₹1,500. The balance becomes ₹500.

b) Credit Card

- A card that lets you borrow money up to a limit.
- You pay later (usually at the end of the month).
- Useful for online purchases and emergencies—but be careful not to overspend!

Note: If you don't pay your credit card bill on time, you pay extra charges (interest + penalty).

c) Prepaid Card

- Like a gift card—load money in advance and spend it.
- Not linked to your bank account.

4. Cheques and Passbooks – Paper Banking Tools

Even with digital options, traditional tools are still used.

a) Cheque

- A written order telling your bank to pay someone a specific amount.
- Used for large transactions or formal payments.
- Needs to be signed and properly filled.

Safety Tip: Never sign a blank cheque!

b) Passbook

- A booklet that records your account transactions.
- Mostly used in savings accounts.

5. ATMs – Anytime, Anywhere Cash

ATM stands for Automated Teller Machine. It's a machine where you can:

- Withdraw cash
- Check account balance
- Print mini statements
- Transfer funds (in some ATMs)

You need a debit card and a PIN (Personal Identification Number) to use it.

Tip: Never share your PIN with anyone!

6. Digital Services – Banking at Your Fingertips

The world of banking has changed rapidly with technology. Now you can do almost everything on your phone or laptop.

a) Mobile Banking

- Use the bank's app to check your balance, transfer money, or pay bills.
- Easy and fast.

b) Internet Banking / Net Banking

- Log into your bank's website to manage your money.

c) UPI (Unified Payments Interface)

- Send or receive money instantly using just a mobile number or UPI ID.
- **Examples:** Google Pay, PhonePe, Paytm, BHIM

Example: Ananya sends ₹500 to her friend instantly using UPI after a group dinner.

7. QR Code and Contactless Payments

• QR codes let you scan and pay with your phone—great for shops and stalls.
• Contactless cards can be tapped on machines without inserting.

Look for the wave icon on cards for contactless features.

8. Insurance and Investment Products

Banks don't just help with saving and borrowing—they can help you grow and protect your money.

a) Insurance
• Banks tie up with insurance companies to offer life, health, and vehicle insurance.
b) Mutual Funds
• Invest in a mix of stocks and bonds through bank-assisted platforms.
c) Sovereign Gold Bonds
• A digital way to invest in gold without buying it physically.

Activity: Match the Service

Service	Description
Savings Account	A. Written payment order
ATM	B. Used to withdraw money anytime
Credit Card	C. Borrowed money to spend now, repay later
Cheque	D. Earn interest and store money safely

Answer:

Savings Account – D

ATM – B

Credit Card – C

Cheque – A

Think & Reflect

- Why is it safer to use a debit card than carrying cash?
- Have you or your parents ever used a cheque? For what purpose?
- Which banking service do you think you'll use the most?

Let's Revise

- Bank accounts are for saving, spending, or investing money.
- Loans help us pay for big expenses like homes or education.
- Cards make transactions cashless and easier.
- ATMs and Cheques are physical tools, while UPI and mobile apps are digital.
- Banks also offer insurance and investment options.

Chapter 5

Digital Banking Revolution in India

Imagine sending money to your friend in 5 seconds. Paying for snacks using just a QR code. Or checking your account balance at midnight from your bed. Welcome to the world of digital banking—fast, easy, and available 24/7!

This chapter explores how India became a global leader in digital payments, the technologies behind it, and how it's changing the way we use banks forever.

1. What is Digital Banking?

Digital banking means accessing banking services using the internet, mobile phones, or other electronic devices—without needing to visit a bank branch.

It includes:

- Internet banking
- Mobile banking apps
- UPI (Unified Payments Interface)

- QR code payments
- Contactless cards
- ATM & POS (Point-of-Sale) services

Why it matters:
Digital banking makes banking faster, safer, and more inclusive. It allows people in remote villages and crowded cities alike to manage their money with a simple smartphone.

2. How It All Started

India's digital banking journey began in the 1990s with the introduction of ATMs and internet banking.

But the real revolution began in the 2010s with:
- Launch of UPI (2016)
- Digital India mission (2015)
- Growth of smartphones and cheap internet

***Fact*:** India now does more digital transactions per month than any other country in the world!

3. What Is UPI and How Does It Work?

UPI (Unified Payments Interface) is India's game-changing digital payment system created by the NPCI (National Payments Corporation of India).

It allows you to:
- Send and receive money instantly
- Pay bills
- Scan QR codes
- Check bank balances

All this using just your mobile number and UPI PIN—no IFSC codes or long bank details needed.

UPI Features:

- 24x7 availability
- Zero charges for most transactions
- Works across multiple banks and apps
- Supports auto-pay for subscriptions and bills

***Example*:** Ritu pays her tuition fees via UPI using her Paytm app. The money reaches the college bank account in seconds!

4. Other Digital Payment Systems

Method	What It Does	Used For
NEFT (National Electronic Funds Transfer)	Transfers money in batches during banking hours	Salary, bills
RTGS (Real Time Gross Settlement)	Transfers large amounts (₹2 lakhs and above) instantly	Big business deals
IMPS (Immediate Payment Service)	24x7 money transfer, instant	Quick personal transfers
AePS (Aadhaar Enabled Payment System)	Uses Aadhaar number and fingerprint to access bank services	Rural ATM alternative

Did You Know? IMPS was launched in India in 2010, before many countries even had instant money transfer!

5. Mobile Banking Apps

Almost every major bank in India has its own mobile app:

- SBI YONO – for shopping, loans, and banking in one app
- HDFC Bank MobileBanking
- ICICI iMobile

- Kotak 811
- Airtel Payments Bank, Paytm Payments Bank

These apps let you:
- Open bank accounts
- Apply for loans
- Pay bills
- View passbooks
- Invest in mutual funds or insurance

Example: Aman checks his account balance, books a movie ticket, and pays his phone bill—all from his bank app!

6. QR Codes and Contactless Payments

Have you seen the square code at shops that says "Scan to Pay"? That's a QR Code—Quick Response Code.
You open your UPI app, scan it, enter the amount, and payment is done in seconds.

Benefits:
- No cash needed
- Safe and touchless
- Great for small vendors and shopkeepers

Case Study: A fruit seller in Varanasi saw a 30% increase in customers after accepting UPI QR payments. Now even buyers without cash stop by!

7. Role of NPCI and India Stack

NPCI (National Payments Corporation of India)

The brain behind:
- UPI

- RuPay cards
- AePS
- Bharat BillPay

India Stack

A set of digital tools that includes:
- Aadhaar (identity)
- e-KYC (paperless verification)
- UPI (cashless transactions)
- DigiLocker (digital documents)

Together, these tools made India the world's leading digital public infrastructure nation.

8. How Digital Banking Helps Small Businesses

- **Instant Payments**: Shopkeepers get money instantly via UPI.
- **Loan Access**: Banks use digital history to offer loans to small vendors.
- **Less Cash Handling**: Reduces theft and counting errors.
- **Customer Reach**: Accepting digital payments means more customers.

Real Impact: Kirana stores in Tier-2 cities saw increased revenue after adopting UPI and QR payments.

9. Is Digital Banking Safe?

Yes, but only if used wisely.

Safety Measures:
- Two-factor authentication
- UPI PIN
- Biometric login

- End-to-end encryption

Tips for Safe Digital Banking:

- Never share OTPs or UPI PINs
- Avoid using public Wi-Fi for banking
- Always log out after using apps
- Report suspicious activity to your bank immediately

Remember: Your bank will NEVER ask for your OTP or password over call or SMS.

Activity: Think & Reflect

1. Have you or your family used UPI? What was the experience like?
2. Why is QR code payment better for small shops than credit cards?
3. Imagine you are building your own digital payment app. What features would you include?

Vocabulary Builder

Term	Meaning
UPI	Unified Payments Interface – India's instant money transfer system
IMPS	Immediate Payment Service – 24/7 instant transfer
QR Code	Scannable code for digital payments
Digital Wallet	App to store money for online use
NPCI	Organization that manages India's digital payment systems

Let's Revise

- Digital banking means banking through phones, computers, or ATMs.
- India's UPI is one of the fastest and safest payment systems globally.
- Apps like Paytm, PhonePe, BHIM, GPay help users pay instantly.
- QR codes make it easy for small vendors to accept payments.
- Always follow cyber safety rules to stay protected online.

✔ With digital banking, the bank is no longer a building. It's now in your pocket. And as a student of tomorrow, you're already a part of India's financial transformation.

Chapter 6

RBI

India's Banker to the Government

Let's Begin

Have you ever wondered who prints the money in your wallet or decides how much interest you earn on your savings? Behind the scenes, one powerful institution takes care of all this — The Reserve Bank of India, also known as the RBI.

In this chapter, we'll explore how the RBI works, its major functions, and how its decisions affect our daily lives. Get ready to meet the "bank of banks" and the financial guardian of India!

1. What is the RBI?

The Reserve Bank of India (RBI) is India's central bank — the topmost financial authority in the country. It was established on 1st April 1935 under the RBI Act, 1934, and was nationalised in 1949.

Key Facts:

- **Headquarters:** Mumbai
- **Current Governor** (as of 2025): Shaktikanta Das
- **Owned by**: Government of India
- **Logo**: A tiger under a palm tree

Think of the RBI as the captain of India's financial ship — it keeps the banking system steady and smooth.

2. Why Do We Need a Central Bank?

Without a central bank like the RBI:

- Different banks could create their own rules.
- Money supply could be mismanaged.
- Inflation could rise uncontrollably.
- People might lose trust in the financial system.

The RBI creates stability, trust, and control in the banking ecosystem.

3. Major Functions of the RBI

Let's break down the RBI's important roles in a simple way:

1. Issuer of Currency

The RBI is the only authority allowed to print currency notes in India (except ₹1, which is issued by the Ministry of Finance).

- It ensures that there is enough money in circulation.
- It also withdraws damaged or fake currency from the system.

Next time you hold a ₹100 note, look at the signature — it's signed by the RBI Governor!

2. Banker to the Government

RBI manages the finances of both:

- Central Government
- State Governments

It collects taxes, manages public debt, and even handles government salary accounts — just like your bank does for you!

3. Banker to Banks

The RBI acts as a bank for all other banks in India:

- Provides loans to banks when needed
- Maintains accounts of banks
- Clears inter-bank transactions

Just like you keep your money in a bank, banks keep their money with the RBI.

4. Regulator of the Banking System

The RBI sets rules for:

- How much money banks must keep in reserve (CRR & SLR)
- How much they can lend
- How to protect customer deposits

If a bank is in trouble or breaks rules, the RBI can investigate or even cancel its license.

5. Controller of Inflation and Interest Rates

The RBI controls inflation and money supply using tools like:

- **Repo Rate:** The interest rate at which RBI lends to banks
- **Reverse Repo Rate:** The rate at which RBI borrows from banks

When inflation is high → RBI increases repo rate → loans become costlier → people borrow less → prices drop
When economy is slow → RBI reduces repo rate → loans become

cheaper → spending increases → economy grows

6. Foreign Exchange Manager

RBI controls the buying and selling of foreign currency and maintains India's forex reserves.
It keeps the Indian Rupee stable in the global market through a system called managed float.

7. Promoter of Financial Inclusion

RBI ensures banking services reach rural, remote, and poor sections of society.

It supports:
- Banking correspondents
- Basic savings accounts
- Priority sector lending
- Financial literacy drives

RBI is working to make banking accessible to every Indian, not just the wealthy or urban.

4. Real-Life Impact of RBI Decisions

Let's understand how RBI decisions touch your daily life:

RBI Action	Impact on You
Changes Repo Rate	Your EMIs go up or down
Prints new currency	You get fresh notes and coins
Cracks down on fraud	Your online banking becomes safer
Promotes digital payments	You can use UPI, Paytm, PhonePe easily

Gives license to new banks	More choices for banking and better services

Example: When RBI reduced the repo rate in 2020, millions of people got cheaper home loans, boosting the housing sector.

5. Important RBI Tools – Explained Simply

Term	Meaning
CRR	Cash Reserve Ratio – money banks must keep with RBI
SLR	Statutory Liquidity Ratio – government bonds banks must hold
Repo Rate	Rate at which RBI lends to banks
Reverse Repo	Rate at which RBI borrows from banks
MSF	Marginal Standing Facility – emergency lending option for banks

Monetary Policy Policy to control money supply and inflation in the economy

These tools help RBI steer the economy like a pilot flies a plane.

6. Activity: If I Were the RBI Governor

Imagine you are the RBI Governor. What decisions would you make in the following situations?

- Inflation is very high – What will you do with the repo rate?
- Digital frauds are increasing – What safety steps will you announce?
- A new private bank wants to open – What rules will you check?

Write your answers in 100 words each and discuss in class!

Vocabulary Builder

Word	Simple Meaning
Inflation	Rise in prices of goods and services
Currency	Official money issued by the government
Central Bank	The top bank that controls other banks
Repo Rate	Interest rate RBI charges banks for loans
Monetary Policy	Decisions that control money and prices

RBI in the News – Real Examples

• **2023:** RBI launched the Digital Rupee, a central bank digital currency.

• **2022:** RBI fined a private bank ₹2 crore for not following loan norms.

• **2021:** RBI announced guidelines for digital lending apps to protect customers.

• **2020:** Repo rate reduced to boost economy during COVID-19 lockdown.

These news updates show how active and responsive RBI is to economic changes.

Let's Revise

- RBI is India's central bank, created in 1935.
- It prints money, controls banks, manages inflation, and supports the economy.
- RBI uses tools like repo rate, CRR, and SLR to regulate the system.
- Its decisions impact your loans, savings, and digital banking.
- RBI promotes safe, inclusive, and modern banking for all.

Key Takeaway:
The RBI is like a powerful referee on the banking field — ensuring fairness, safety, and balance in the economy.

Chapter 7

How to Open and Use a Bank Account

Let's Begin

Have you ever wondered what it takes to open a bank account or how to use it smartly? This chapter is your complete guide! It will walk you through how banks work for you — from your first visit to the branch or app to managing your money safely and wisely.
A bank account is more than just a place to keep your money — it's your first step toward financial independence.

1. What is a Bank Account?

A bank account is like your personal money locker in a bank. You deposit your money, and the bank keeps it safe. You can withdraw it when you need it, earn interest on your savings, and even pay bills or shop online.
There are different types of accounts for different needs:

Type of Account	Purpose
Savings Account	For regular saving and earning interest
Current Account	For businesses with frequent transactions
Fixed Deposit (FD)	For locking your money and earning higher interest
Recurring Deposit (RD)	For monthly saving with interest
Student Account	Special accounts for young people with no fees

Did you know? Most teenagers can open a student account with a guardian, and start learning money skills early!

2. Steps to Open a Bank Account

Whether you walk into a branch or do it online, here's a simple step-by-step process:

Step 1: Choose the Right Bank and Account Type
• Research banks like SBI, HDFC, ICICI, Axis Bank, or even digital banks like Fi or Paytm.
• Decide the type of account that suits your needs.

Step 2: Fill Out the Application Form
• You can fill the form physically at a bank or online via the bank's website or app.
• The form will ask for your name, address, age, occupation, and nominee details.

Step 3: Complete Your KYC (Know Your Customer)
KYC is a legal step where you verify your identity.
You need:
• ID Proof (Aadhaar Card, PAN Card, Passport)

• Address Proof (Electricity Bill, Ration Card, etc.)
• Photograph
• Signature or thumbprint

Tip: If you're below 18, your parent or guardian will co-sign and provide their documents.

Step 4: Deposit Money
• You must deposit a minimum balance (e.g., ₹500 or ₹1,000) depending on the bank.
• Some zero-balance accounts don't need this.

Step 5: Receive Your Welcome Kit
You will receive:
• Passbook
• ATM/Debit Card
• Cheque Book (optional)
• Account Number

Your bank account is now active!

3. How to Use Your Bank Account

Once your account is open, here are the things you can do:
Deposit and Withdraw Money
• Use bank branches, ATMs, or cash deposit machines.
• Mobile apps allow instant transfers (IMPS, UPI, NEFT).

Send and Receive Payments
• Pay your school fees or mobile bills.
• Send birthday gifts to friends through UPI!
• Get scholarship money or salary directly in your account.
Track Your Balance

Use:
- SMS alerts
- Mobile apps
- Internet banking
- Mini statements from ATMs

Always check for suspicious transactions and report them.

Earn Interest
- Most savings accounts offer 2.5%–4% interest per annum.
- Some digital accounts even offer higher rates.

4. Understanding Your Bank Statement

A bank statement is a document that lists:
- Every time money came in (credit)
- Every time money went out (debit)
- Your account balance after each transaction

Date	Description	Amount	Type	Balance
01/07/25	UPI transfer from Ankit	₹500	Credit	₹1,500
02/07/25	ATM Withdrawal	₹200	Debit	₹1,300
03/07/25	Zomato – Lunch Order	₹150	Debit	₹1,150

Tip: Review your statement monthly to track spending and spot errors.

5. ATM Safety & Digital Tips

ATMs are convenient, but here's how to use them safely:
- Never share your PIN with anyone.

• Cover the keypad when entering the PIN.
• If the ATM looks tampered, avoid using it.
• Don't let strangers "help" you.

Digital Safety Tips:
• Use strong passwords and change them regularly.
• Use official banking apps only.
• Don't click on suspicious SMS or email links.
• Enable 2-factor authentication for login and transactions.

6. Common Bank Charges You Should Know

Some bank services come with fees. Know them to avoid surprises:

Service	Possible Charges
Minimum Balance Penalty	If your balance falls below limit
ATM Withdrawal (after limit)	₹10–20 per transaction
SMS Alerts	₹15–30 quarterly (some banks)
Cheque Bounce	₹150–300
Statement Print	₹50 per request

Always read the terms and conditions when opening an account.

7. Activity: Practice Filling a Bank Form

Create a mock account opening form with the following fields:
• **Name:** ______________________
• **Date of Birth:** ________________
• **Aadhaar Number:** ______________
• **PAN Number:** _________________
• **Mobile Number:** _______________
• **Account Type (Tick):** [ ] Savings [ ] Student [ ] FD

- **Nominee Name:** ___________________
- **Signature:** _______________________

Now try filling it yourself and share with your teacher or classmate for feedback!

8. Vocabulary Builder

Term	Meaning
KYC	Know Your Customer – ID verification process
ATM	Automated Teller Machine – for cash withdrawal
Passbook	A record book of your account's transactions
UPI	Unified Payments Interface – instant payment system
Interest	Money you earn for keeping money in the bank
Debit Card	A card to withdraw money or shop using your account

9. Real-World Example: Priya's First Account

Priya is 16 and wants to open a student savings account. She visits the bank with her father and Aadhaar Card. They choose a zero-balance account with a debit card. Within 2 days, she gets her account number and starts saving her pocket money. She now uses UPI to pay for stationery and track her balance from her mobile. Priya says, "It's fun and empowering to manage my money. I feel like an adult!"

Let’s Revise

- A bank account helps you save, spend, and grow your money safely.
- Opening an account involves choosing a bank, filling forms, doing KYC, and depositing money.
- You can track transactions, earn interest, and pay digitally.
- Safety is key — protect your PIN and use official apps only.
- Knowing your bank statement and charges helps you be a smart account holder.

Chapter 8

Banking Safely

Know Your Rights

In today's world of digital money, ATMs, mobile banking, and UPI payments, banking is easier than ever — but also comes with risks. As a young customer, it's important to not just know how to use banking services, but also how to stay safe and understand your rights.
This chapter will help you learn how to avoid fraud, protect your money, and know what to do when something goes wrong. Smart banking = Safe banking!

1. Why Banking Safety Matters

Imagine someone hacks your bank app and transfers your money. Or your debit card gets cloned and misused. These things are possible if you're not alert.

Banking safety is about:

• Keeping your money and information secure

• Avoiding scams and frauds
• Knowing how to react quickly in case of mistakes or threats
In India, millions of people use digital banking.

That's why RBI and banks have strong guidelines to protect customers. But YOU are your first line of defence.

2. Your Rights as a Bank Customer

Yes, as a customer — even a student — you have rights protected by the RBI.

Here are the main ones:

Right	What It Means
Right to Fair Treatment	No discrimination based on age, gender, religion, or location
Right to Information	You must get full information on charges, interest, and products
Right to Privacy	Your personal and financial data must be kept confidential
Right to Transparency	Charges, terms and conditions must be clearly explained
Right to Grievance Redressal	If something goes wrong, you can file a complaint with the bank or RBI
Right to Easy Account Closure	You can close your account anytime without unfair barriers

Banks are expected to communicate in simple language and give you time to read terms before you sign.

3. Safe Banking Practices – Offline and Online

At the Bank Branch

- Don't share your PIN or account number with strangers
- Count your cash before leaving the counter
- Don't sign blank cheques or forms
- Carry your passbook and ID safely

At the ATM

- Use ATMs in well-lit, secure locations
- Shield the keypad while entering your PIN
- Never accept help from strangers at ATMs
- Take your card and receipt before leaving

On Mobile and Net Banking

- Install only official bank apps from the Play Store or App Store
- Use strong passwords and change them regularly
- Don't share OTPs or passwords
- Log out after every banking session
- Turn on SMS/email alerts for all transactions

Beware of phishing — fake emails or messages pretending to be from banks. They might ask you to "update KYC" or "verify your account" and steal your info.

4. Types of Banking Frauds to Watch Out For

Fraudsters are getting smarter. You should know how they operate:

Type of Fraud	How It Works	How to Stay Safe
Phishing	Fake emails/SMS asking for account or card details	Never click suspicious links or share details

SIM Swap	Fraudsters clone your mobile SIM to get OTPs	Contact your mobile provider if your SIM stops working suddenly
ATM Skimming	Devices fitted on ATMs steal your card data	Inspect ATM machines for unusual devices
Vishing	Fraud calls pretending to be from your bank	Banks never ask for OTPs over phone — hang up
UPI Scams	Scammers trick you into scanning a QR code to “receive” money	Remember: you only scan when paying, not receiving!

Report frauds immediately to your bank and on the Cyber Crime portal: https://cybercrime.gov.in

5. What to Do If Something Goes Wrong

\If you lose money or notice suspicious activity:

1. Call your bank’s toll-free number immediately
2. Block your debit/credit card or mobile banking account
3. Register a complaint with your bank
4. If unresolved, complain to RBI Ombudsman

RBI Banking Ombudsman:

This is a senior RBI officer who handles complaints. You can submit a complaint online at:
https://cms.rbi.org.in
The bank must reply within 30 days.

6. Real-World Example – Learning from Mistakes

Aarav’s Story

Aarav, a 17-year-old, got a call from someone pretending to be from his bank. They said there was a "security update" and asked for his debit card details and OTP. Aarav shared them, and ₹7,500 was deducted from his account.
He panicked but then called his bank and blocked his card. He also registered a cyber fraud complaint online and followed up regularly.

The lesson: Aarav acted late, but his quick reaction reduced the damage. NEVER share OTPs with anyone!

7. Tools for Secure Banking

Here are tools and settings you can enable:

- Transaction Alerts – Get SMS or email for every transaction
- Two-Factor Authentication – Required for logins and payments
- Virtual Debit Cards – Safer for online purchases
- Set Spending Limits – Control how much can be spent or withdrawn
- UPI PIN Reset – If compromised, change it immediately via the app

Remember: YOU are the password to your money.

8. Know Your Rights: Sample Scenario Quiz

Let's test your understanding with a few examples:

Situation 1:
You opened a student savings account and didn't understand the hidden SMS alert fee.
Your Right?
→ Right to Transparent Information

Situation 2:
Your online transaction failed, but the money was deducted.

What should you do?
→ Report it to the bank and get a refund in 7 working days.

Situation 3:
You receive a link to "update your KYC" and it asks for your PAN and Aadhaar.
What now?
→ Don't click. It's a phishing scam. Report it!

9. Vocabulary Builder

Term	Meaning
OTP	One-Time Password for verifying transactions
Phishing	Tricking you into revealing confidential data
Ombudsman	RBI-appointed officer for customer complaint redressal

Card Skimming Stealing card data from ATM or POS machine
Vishing Fraud call pretending to be from a bank

Let's Reflect

Imagine you got your first salary. You deposited it in your bank account. But one day, you receive a fake message saying you've won ₹1 lakh, and they ask for your account details.

What would you do?
A smart customer:
- Doesn't fall for the trap
- Reports the number
- Blocks suspicious accounts

That's what financial awareness looks like.

Let's Revise

- You have rights as a bank customer – privacy, fair treatment, complaint redressal.
- Always follow safe banking habits offline and online.
- Know how to spot common frauds and react fast.
- RBI offers help through the Banking Ombudsman.
- The more aware you are, the safer your money is!

Key Takeaway:

Banking is not just about money — it's about trust and safety. Learn to protect your financial information, know your rights, and be a smart, alert, and confident customer.

Chapter 9

Future of Banking in India

The world is changing fast — and so is banking! From long queues at the bank counter to instant mobile payments, we've already come a long way. But what's next?

In this chapter, you'll explore what the future of banking in India might look like —

powered by artificial intelligence, digital currencies, cashless systems, and even virtual reality.
You'll learn how young people like you can shape this future through ideas, innovation, and awareness.

1. From Banking 1.0 to Banking 5.0 – What Does That Mean?

Banking has evolved in phases:

Banking 1.0	Traditional branch banking with in-person visits and passbooks (pre-1960s)
Banking 2.0	ATMs, debit/credit cards, basic computerization (1960s–1980s)
Banking 3.0	Internet and mobile banking, online transfers (1990s–2010s)
Banking 4.0	Open banking, UPI, digital wallets, app-based banking (2010s–2020s)
Banking 5.0	AI, blockchain, biometric security, digital currencies (emerging now and beyond)

We are now entering the Banking 5.0 era — more digital, more personal, and more intelligent.

2. Role of Artificial Intelligence (AI) in Banking

AI is no longer science fiction. It's becoming your financial buddy.

Here's how banks will use AI:

• **AI Chatbots:** You can ask your bank app, "How much did I spend this week?" and get an instant answer.

• **Spending Insights:** AI will analyse your habits and say, "Hey, you're overspending on food delivery!"

• **Voice Banking:** Just say "Send ₹500 to Mom" — and it will do it (with secure checks).

• **Fraud Detection:** AI
systems will spot fraud patterns in milliseconds and block suspicious transactions.

Real Example: SBI's YONO app and HDFC's Eva chatbot are already using AI to assist customers 24x7.

3. Digital Rupee and Central Bank Digital Currencies (CBDCs)

Heard about "crypto"? Well, here's a government-backed version — the Digital Rupee.
India's Digital Rupee (e₹) is issued by the RBI, not a private

company. It's a new form of money that:

- Exists only in digital format
- Is safe and traceable
- Can be used for both retail (daily use) and wholesale (banking between banks)

Benefits of Digital Rupee:

- No need to print physical notes = environment-friendly
- Instant transfers = no delays
- Lower risk of fake currency
- More transparency in transactions

Think of it as "Digital Cash in your phone," directly from the Reserve Bank.

4. Hyper-Personalised Banking Experiences

In the future, banking will be like your playlist – customised for you.

How?

- Your bank will offer tailored savings plans based on your income and spending
- Investment advice will match your goals (like saving for college or travel)
- Loan offers will auto-calculate based on your credit profile

Your banking app will understand YOU — your needs, your habits, and your goals.

5. Embedded Finance – Banking Everywhere

Banking will become so smooth, you won't even notice it.
• You'll be able to make a payment while chatting on WhatsApp
• Buy-now-pay-later options will be available in every shopping app
• Loan approvals will happen inside education or e-commerce apps

This is Embedded Finance — banking services built inside apps you already use.

Example: Swiggy may offer instant credit at checkout, or Zomato may let you split bills through UPI.

6. Better Security – Biometrics and Beyond

As banking gets more digital, security is the key.

Coming soon:
• **Face Recognition:** Use your face to log into your banking app.
• **Fingerprint Authentication:** Already in use, but will become standard for payments.
• **Behavioural Security:** The way you type or swipe will help detect fraud!

Also, banks will invest heavily in cybersecurity tools to protect you from hackers, data theft, and phishing.

7. FinTech and Innovation Labs

India is a FinTech superpower!
FinTech = Financial Technology

Startups are building:
• New ways to save
• Smarter insurance apps

• Robo-advisors for investing
• Loan marketplaces

Banks are also starting innovation labs to test futuristic ideas.

Did you know? India has over 8,000 FinTech companies. UPI, BHIM, Paytm, Zerodha, PhonePe — all are FinTechs!
You could even intern or work in one after school!

8. Green Banking and Sustainability

As climate change becomes a concern, banks will support:
• **Green Loans:** Lower-interest loans for solar panels, EVs, and energy-saving homes
• **Paperless Banking:** Reducing waste and saving trees
• **Eco Rewards:** Cashback and offers for choosing eco-friendly products
Future banking = Smart + Safe + Sustainable

9. Virtual Reality (VR) Banking – The 3D Bank!

This might sound like a game, but VR is entering finance.

Imagine:
• Walking into a virtual bank branch using a headset
• Talking to a virtual financial advisor in 3D
• Seeing your money visualised as graphs and animations in a virtual room
This is still experimental, but possible very soon!

10. You and the Future of Banking

You may wonder: "I'm just a student — how do I fit into all this?"
Here's how:
• You are the next generation of banking users

• Your needs and habits shape how banks will operate
• You might design apps, build secure payment tools, or create awareness

Future bankers need:
• Creativity
• Financial literacy
• Tech skills
• Ethics and empathy

You could become a FinTech founder, cybersecurity expert, or even the next RBI Governor!

Activity: Imagine Your Own Bank App

Design a futuristic bank app on paper or using a drawing tool.

Think of:
• What features it will have (voice pay? investment tips?)
• What age group it will serve (kids? teens? senior citizens?)
• What its name, logo, and colors will be

Present your idea in class or to friends — and see who comes up with the coolest future bank!

Let's Revise

• Banking 5.0 = AI, digital rupee, smart banking experiences
• The Digital Rupee (CBDC) is India's new digital currency
• Banks will use AI and biometrics to make banking easier and safer
• Embedded Finance will bring banking into everyday apps
• Students like you will lead the future of smart, secure, and inclusive banking!

Final Takeaway:

The future of banking in India is full of opportunity — smarter, faster, and greener. As India becomes a global digital leader, its banking system is evolving with it. And YOU are at the center of this change.

Chapter 10

Careers in Banking and FinTech

Have you ever imagined yourself working in a big bank office, approving loans, or designing the next cool banking app? The world of banking and financial technology (FinTech) offers exciting, stable, and high-paying careers — and many of these opportunities are now open to young, tech-savvy students like you.
This chapter will help you explore the different types of careers in banking and FinTech, the skills you need, and how to prepare for them.

1. Traditional Careers in Banking

Let's start with the classic roles that have existed for decades in banks:
Bank Clerk or Teller
• The first point of contact at a bank branch.
• Handles cash deposits, withdrawals, cheques, and queries.
• Requires good communication and math skills.

Loan Officer

- Evaluates and approves loan applications (like home loans, car loans, etc.).
- Works with both individuals and businesses.
- Needs analytical thinking and decision-making skills.

Branch Manager

- In charge of managing the entire bank branch.
- Handles staff, operations, customer service, and performance.
- Usually promoted after years of experience.

Relationship Manager

- Builds relationships with key customers.
- Helps them with investment, insurance, and financial advice.
- Needs excellent communication and trust-building abilities.

2. Government Banking Jobs

Want to work in public sector banks like SBI or RBI? Here are some popular exams:

IBPS PO (Probationary Officer)

- For jobs in banks like Punjab National Bank, Bank of Baroda, etc.
- Requires graduation and clearing an entrance exam.

SBI PO

- Prestigious officer-level post in State Bank of India.
- Conducted separately by SBI.

RBI Grade B

- Officer post at the Reserve Bank of India.
- Highly respected, well-paid, and competitive.

Clerical Exams (IBPS Clerk, SBI Clerk)

- Entry-level roles in bank branches.

These exams test your English, reasoning, math, and general knowledge. Coaching, practice, and dedication are key.

3. New-Age Careers in FinTech

Today, banks are becoming tech companies. This means there are many modern roles that combine finance with technology.

Here are some exciting options:

Cybersecurity Specialist
- Protects customer data and digital banking systems.
- Involves coding, ethical hacking, and security analysis.

UI/UX Designer
- Designs easy-to-use and attractive banking apps.
- Works on how the app looks and feels to the user.

Data Analyst / Risk Analyst
- Studies customer data to understand patterns and risks.
- Helps banks decide who to give loans to or where to invest.

Product Manager (Banking Apps)
- Plans and launches digital banking products like mobile apps or UPI systems.
- Coordinates between tech, design, and marketing teams.

Blockchain Developer
- Builds secure and transparent systems using blockchain.
- In demand due to the rise of digital rupee and crypto-like technologies.

Companies hiring for these roles: Paytm, Razorpay, PhonePe, CRED, Zerodha, Google Pay, etc.

4. Skills You Need for a Career in Banking & FinTech

Whether you want to be a branch officer or a digital banking innovator,

You'll need a mix of core and soft skills:

Skill	Why It's Important
Communication	Deal with customers, explain products clearly
Analytical thinking	Solve financial problems, analyse reports
Computer literacy	Use banking software, apps, and tools
Ethics & integrity	Handle money responsibly
Teamwork	Collaborate in banks and startups
Tech-savviness	Understand digital trends, fintech tools
Creativity & innovation	Think of new services and customer experiences

You can start building these skills through:
- School projects
- Online finance games and simulators
- Internships or shadowing at a bank
- Tech competitions or coding bootcamps

5. Courses and Certifications That Help

If you're serious about a banking career, here are some useful study paths:

Undergraduate Degrees
- B.Com (Banking & Finance)
- BBA (Banking/Finance)

• B.Tech (Computer Science or FinTech specialisation)
• BA in Economics or Mathematics

Postgraduate Degrees
• MBA in Finance – great for high-paying roles
• PGDM in Banking and Financial Services – focused on BFSI sector

Professional Certifications
• NISM (National Institute of Securities Markets) – for investment jobs
• IIBF (Indian Institute of Banking and Finance) – offers JAIIB, CAIIB
• FRM (Financial Risk Manager) – for risk management
• CFA (Chartered Financial Analyst) – for global finance careers
• Certified FinTech Professional – available from global ed-tech platforms

Many online platforms like Coursera, edX, and NSE Academy offer FinTech courses.

6. Global Opportunities

Banking and FinTech are global. Once you gain skills and experience, you can work in:
• International banks (HSBC, Citi, JP Morgan)
• Global FinTech firms (Stripe, Revolut, Wise)
• International markets (UAE, Singapore, UK, Canada)

Learning an extra language (like German, Mandarin, or Spanish) and understanding global finance norms can boost your prospects.

7. Real Career Journeys – Indian Role Models

Arundhati Bhattacharya
• First woman Chairperson of SBI.

• Started as a probationary officer and rose to the top!

Nandan Nilekani
• Co-founder of Infosys and key architect of Aadhaar and UPI.
• Bridged the gap between tech and finance.

Harshil Mathur (CEO, Razorpay)
• Built a FinTech unicorn from scratch with his friend.
• Started with a simple idea: making digital payments easier for businesses.

These role models prove that hard work + vision can take you to the top — whether in public banks or modern FinTechs.

Activity: What Banking Career Suits You?

Pick the statement that best describes you:

If You Like...	Career Options
Talking to people, solving their problems	Bank teller, relationship manager
Analysing data and spotting trends	Risk analyst, data scientist
Creating apps and digital tools	App developer, UI/UX designer
Thinking of innovative money-saving ideas	Product manager, fintech founder
Working for the government and public service	SBI PO, RBI Grade B officer

Make a list of careers that interest you and start researching what qualifications and skills they need!

Let's Revise

• Banking and FinTech careers include both traditional and digital roles.
• Government jobs like IBPS PO, SBI Clerk, and RBI Officer are highly competitive.
• FinTech offers jobs in design, coding, cybersecurity, and data analysis.

• **Key skills:** Communication, tech knowledge, ethics, analysis.

• **Study options:** B.Com, MBA, IIBF, CFA, FinTech certifications.
• Role models like Arundhati Bhattacharya and Nandan Nilekani show the range of career possibilities.

Final Takeaway:

Banking is not just about money — it's about opportunity, innovation, and trust. Whether you dream of working in a traditional branch or launching a FinTech startup, the future is wide open. Start early, stay curious, and you could be the next big name in banking!

Chapter 11

Start Young

Building Banking Habits

Have you ever saved money in a piggy bank? Bought a gift for someone using your pocket money? Or opened a student account in a bank? Congratulations — you've already taken your first steps into the world of banking!
In this chapter, we'll show you how to build smart money habits early in life. These small habits, when practiced regularly, can lead to a future where you feel confident about saving, spending, and managing money wisely.

1. Start with Saving

Saving is the most basic and essential banking habit. It teaches patience, discipline, and planning.

Why Save?
• To buy something you really want (phone, cycle, gifts)

• For emergencies or unexpected needs
• To learn how to manage money and not spend everything you get

Where to Start?
• Use a piggy bank or savings jar for coins and notes.
• Track your savings weekly.
• **Set a goal:** "I want to save ₹500 in two months."

Tip: Even saving ₹10 per day adds up to ₹3,650 in a year!

2. Explore Student and Teen Bank Accounts

As you grow older, you can move from a piggy bank to a real bank account designed for students or minors.

What is a Minor Bank Account?
• A savings account for children below 18.
• Opened jointly with a parent or guardian.
• Comes with a debit card and mobile banking access (limited use).

Benefits:
• Teaches you how real banks work.
• Builds the habit of depositing and checking balances.
• Some accounts offer small interest on your savings.

Example: Banks like SBI, ICICI, HDFC, and Kotak offer student accounts with special features and no minimum balance requirements.

3. Budgeting Basics – Plan Before You Spend

Learning how to budget helps you control where your money goes.

How to Budget:
1. Write down all the money you receive in a month (allowance,

gifts, rewards).
2. Make a list of your expenses (snacks, books, mobile recharge, etc.).

3. Divide your money:

- o 50% for needs
- o 30% for wants
- o 20% for savings

Quick Rule: Save first, spend later — not the other way around!

Activity:
Use a notebook or Excel sheet and track your money daily for one week. Find out what you spend most on.

4. Understanding Needs vs. Wants

This is one of the biggest money lessons in life.

Needs	**Wants**
School books, stationery	New phone case
Bus fare, food	Designer shoes
Health, emergency savings	Online games, subscriptions

Prioritize needs before wants. Ask: Do I really need this, or do I just want it?

5. Learn to Deposit and Withdraw

Once you have a bank account:

- Try depositing your birthday money or allowances.
- Use the ATM (with help) to withdraw small amounts.
- Ask your parents to show you a bank statement to track how much money is going in and out.

Remember:

- Never share your ATM PIN or password with anyone.
- Always log out of net banking or mobile apps after use.

6. Get Comfortable with Digital Money

Digital money is here to stay. From paying at the canteen to buying movie tickets — most payments are now digital.

Learn These Basics:

- How UPI apps like PhonePe, Google Pay, Paytm work
- What is OTP and how to use it safely
- How to scan QR codes for payment

Start with small, supervised digital transactions with family.

7. Make Smart Spending Decisions

Think before you spend. Ask:

- Is it worth the price?
- Will I still want this next week?
- Can I get a better deal elsewhere?

Pro tip: Sleep on big decisions. If you still want it the next morning, consider buying it.

8. Track and Analyse Your Spending

Once you start spending, it's important to track your money.

Tools You Can Use:

- A simple notebook
- Mobile notes
- Budgeting apps (with parental help)

At the end of the month, ask:
• How much did I save?
• What did I spend the most on?
• Where can I cut down next month?

9. Keep Your Money Safe – Online & Offline

Money is valuable. Keep it safe from theft, scams, or loss.

Offline Safety:
• Don't carry all your money at once.
• Keep your wallet or piggy bank in a secure place.
• Count your change at shops.

Online Safety:
• Never share passwords, OTPs, or account info.
• Don't click on suspicious links or emails.
• Always use banking apps with two-step verification.
Talk to your parents if something feels suspicious or if you lose money.

10. Build a Good Money Attitude

The way you think about money matters just as much as how you use it.
Be patient – Save before you buy.
Be honest – Don't lie about how you spent money.
Be disciplined – Follow your budget, even when tempted.
Be grateful – Appreciate what you have before wanting more.

11. Reflect: What Will You Do With Your First Salary?

Imagine you've just received your first job salary. What would you do?
Would you:

• Save a part of it?
• Spend it all on gadgets?
• Gift something to your parents?
• Invest in your dreams?

Write a short paragraph titled: "My First Salary – My Plan" and include:
• 3 things you would do with the money
• 1 smart financial decision
• 1 emotional decision

Let's Revise

• Start saving early — even coins matter.
• Open a student account to learn real-world banking.
• Learn to budget: Needs vs. Wants.
• Use digital payments wisely and safely.
• Build a money-positive mindset.

Final Takeaway:

You don't need to be rich to start good banking habits — you just need to start. With smart habits, clear goals, and honest efforts, you can become financially smart and confident before you even leave school.

The earlier you learn to manage money, the more control you'll have over your future.

Glossary of Key Banking Terms

Term	Meaning (Simple Explanation)
Account	A record at a bank where your money is stored and managed.
ATM (Automated Teller Machine)	A machine that lets you withdraw or deposit cash using your debit/ATM card.
Bank Statement	A summary showing all transactions (deposits, withdrawals) in your bank account.
Beneficiary	The person who receives money in a bank transaction.
Cheque	A paper slip used to pay money from one bank account to another.
Collateral	Something valuable (like property or gold) pledged for a loan; it's security for the bank.
Credit Card	A card that lets you borrow money from the bank to pay for purchases, to be repaid later.
Debit Card	A card that takes money directly from your account when you buy something.
Deposit	Putting money into your bank account.
Digital Banking	Using online or mobile platforms to do banking without visiting a branch.
EMI (Equated Monthly Installment)	The fixed monthly amount you pay to repay a loan (includes interest).
FD (Fixed Deposit)	Money kept in the bank for a fixed time period that earns higher interest.

FinTech	Short for "Financial Technology" – companies using tech to offer better financial services.
IFSC Code	A unique code used to identify a specific bank branch during online transfers.
IMPS (Immediate Payment Service)	Real-time money transfer method available 24/7 via mobile or online banking.
Interest	Extra money paid by the bank for keeping your money (savings) or charged on loans.
KYC (Know Your Customer)	A process where banks verify your identity using documents like Aadhaar, PAN, etc.
Loan	Money borrowed from a bank that must be repaid with interest.
Mobile Banking	Doing banking using a smartphone app.
Net Banking	Doing banking through a website using your username and password.
NEFT (National Electronic Funds Transfer)	A way to transfer money from one bank account to another in batches.
NPA (Non-Performing Asset)	A loan that hasn't been repaid for a long time; it's considered bad debt.
OTP (One-Time Password)	A temporary code sent to your phone/ email to approve secure online transactions.
Passbook	A small book that shows a written record of your bank account transactions.

PIN (Personal Identification Number)	A 4- or 6-digit secret number used to access your bank account through ATMs.
Repo Rate	The interest rate at which RBI lends money to commercial banks.
RBI (Reserve Bank of India)	India's central bank that controls money supply, interest rates, and banking regulations.
RTGS (Real-Time Gross Settlement)	A fast method of transferring large amounts of money between banks instantly.
Savings Account	A basic bank account where you can save money and earn interest.
Transaction	Any activity in your bank account – deposit, withdrawal, transfer, etc.
UPI (Unified Payments Interface)	A digital system that lets you instantly transfer money using your phone.
Withdrawal	Taking money out of your bank account.